the Art of HARVEST

Intentional Menus for the Creative Cook

JULIE HOUSER
Celebrity Plant-Based Chef

Carrot Vinaigrette > Recipe pg 87

To the countless souls whose palates I've had the pleasure of pleasing over the last quarter-century, this cookbook is truly a tribute to you. The sacred shared moments around the table, the laughter, the sparkle in your eye, that special place inside and the satisfied sighs have all woven themselves into the fabric of these recipes. To friends who tasted countless trials, provided honest feedback and cheered me on when the kitchen seemed like a chaotic dance floor—your friendship has been the secret ingredient in this culinary journey. This book is way more than a collection of dishes; it's a beautiful celebration of the flavors we've savored together. Thank you for being the secret ingredients that make this culinary journey so special.

Here's to the joy of good food and the wonderful company that makes it even more memorable.

 ISBN: 978-1-962973-81-6
Printed in the United States of America.

EDITOR Mehak Hussain | Little Things Ltd.
DESIGN Krista Murphy | Wishtree Design inc.
PHOTOGRAPHY Sarah Hays | Hays Media Co

TABLE OF CONTENTS

INTRODUCTION

A great menu is like foreplay—it has the capacity to create desire and wonder, to entice a dialogue with your imagination. Throughout my career as a chef, I have always started with building the menu. In fact, for me, the dining experience does not begin without the presence of a captivating menu. Creating the menu and then sharing it early with your guests gives them time to imagine what each dish might taste like. Offering a space to imagine delight is part of the dance. This conversation between our brain and our taste buds, increases the desire for the meal and evokes suspense and excitement that will later enhance every bite.

These seasonal menus require the freshest of produce. The pursuit of ingredients is everything. Visiting local farmer's markets is one of the best ways to ensure you are getting the freshest produce. Get to know your local farmers. They will be your friends—I promise! They will start to let you know when they have something special or perhaps offer you a case of seconds of tomatoes in the middle of the summer. These make the most incredible fresh tomato sauce! They will let you know when the local carrots are in, when they are at the peak of sweet freshness and they will be the star of the show at your dinner party. These gifts are priceless gems–offering the ultimate in fresh, seasonal bounty. Keep in mind, the finished product will only be as delicious as the ingredients themselves.

This book is built around seasonal menus. Feel free to pick and choose recipes in the menu or have some of your favorite folks over to enjoy it in its entirety. Breaking bread with friends, in my opinion, is pretty much the best thing in the world. This is the only time when we can leave our divisions, opinions and troubles at the door, while we all gather around the table to enjoy one another and the bounty of food. This is a sacred place, where we connect over flavors and take time to focus on food and taste, savoring both its ingredients and the shared experience.

My hope is through enjoying this book, you too will become an artist of food, incorporating your own flair and intentions, making these seasonal recipes shine even brighter. Mindfulness and intentionality are important throughout the entire culinary process; from menu writing to ingredient selection to the preparation of the meal and finally, to enjoying the flavors of the finished dishes. These are the best moments in life. I hope this journey into *The Art of Harvest* makes these moments extra special for you and for the people you love to feed.

XO *Jules*

JULIE HOUSER: THE FLOWER CHEF

Julie Houser, a celebrated entrepreneur, celebrity chef and the visionary behind Flower Chef Foods, boasts over 25 years of culinary expertise. Known far and wide as *The Flower Chef* for her delectable farm-to-table feasts, she's earned the admiration of celebrities, diplomats and industry leaders alike.

In 1999, Chef Jules founded Julie Summers Catering in Santa Barbara, rising in popularity as one of the city's premier celebrity chefs. Her innovative, plant-based creations, crafted from locally sourced, fresh ingredients, earned her the Pacific Coast Business Times' esteemed *Forty Under 40* award.

Following a move to Seattle in 2004 and a stint as a pharmaceutical sales representative, Chef Jules faced a life changing battle with stage 3 breast cancer in 2011. The experience inspired her to make changes to her lifestyle, including changing to a plant based diet. She was driven to make plant-based eating more enjoyable and more accessible to people. Drawing on her years of culinary expertise, she turned to her kitchen creating a delicious line of innovative hemp seed oil blends called OLA Gourmet. This is her flagship line and marks the birth of her company, Flower Chef Foods.

Beyond her celebrated culinary career, Chef Jules practices yoga and meditation daily. She enjoys painting and spending time with her family in the Pacific Northwest. She resides in Seattle with her psychiatrist husband, Jim, and their two sons, alongside their loyal chocolate lab, Winnie. Armed with a Bachelor of Arts degree in English from the University of California, Santa Barbara. The Flower Chef is poised to take her brand to the global stage, captivating palates worldwide.

THE FLOWER CHEF'S PANTRY

While each of my seasonal menus are centered around fresh, locally sourced produce, I make sure to keep some of these staples on hand at all times. Having a robust pantry offers the canvas and the tools to create a culinary masterpiece. All you need to do is choose your palette of fresh vegetables and herbs and you're ready to go! A perfect plant-based meal awaits.

Pantry Items

Butter and Oil

Plant-Based Butters: typically crafted by blending oils like coconut, soy, or olive oil with emulsifiers and flavoring agents, resulting in a dairy-free alternative that mimics the creamy consistency and taste of traditional butter. For a flavor that more closely resembles rich, European butter, I like to combine two or three different plant based butter brands. This approach works great when making plant based compounded butters as well.

Extra Virgin Olive Oil: extracted from the first cold pressing of olives, delivers a rich and robust flavor profile, featuring a harmonious blend of fruity, peppery, and slightly bitter notes. This rich velvety oil enhances the taste of dishes with a distinctive Mediterranean charm. EVOO is also celebrated for its high levels of monounsaturated fats and antioxidants, promoting heart health and adding a healthful touch to a variety of dishes.

Sesame Oil: derived from sesame seeds, offers a distinct nutty flavor that enhances various dishes. Beyond its culinary appeal, this oil is rich in antioxidants and healthy fats, promoting heart health and reducing inflammation. When offered a choice between toasted or untoasted sesame oil, I always opt for toasted. It is sure to deliver a nuttier, rounder, more full bodied flavor.

OLA Gourmet: Flower Chef Foods' line of gourmet hemp seed oil blends. Each oil marries the best notes of hemp seed oil with other nutrient rich oils making the miraculous hemp seed and its benefits more readily available in our diets. Hemp seed oil on its own tends to be grassy and a little bitter. I like to build these oil blends into recipes in place of their individual counterparts.

Vinegars

Apple Cider Vinegar: renowned for its tangy kick, adds depth and brightness to a variety of dishes, from salads to marinades. Beyond its culinary charm, this elixir is celebrated for potential health benefits, including aiding digestion, stabilizing blood sugar levels, and promoting weight loss. Incorporating apple cider vinegar into your cooking not only elevates flavor but also adds a delicious dose of wellness to your plate.

Balsamic Vinegar: with its sweet and complex flavor profile, offers a velvety touch to dishes, balancing both sweetness and acidity. Its rich, dark color and syrupy consistency add a beautiful glaze to salads, roasted vegetables, and even desserts. The nuanced notes of balsamic vinegar, ranging from fruity to woody, elevate the taste experience, making it a versatile and sophisticated ingredient.

Seasonings

Kosher Salt: using kosher salt in cooking is crucial for achieving well-balanced flavors, as its coarse texture allows for better control and distribution during seasoning. The larger grains of kosher salt also make it easier to pinch, providing both a tactile and intuitive approach to seasoning dishes. Additionally, because kosher salt lacks additives like iodine and anti-caking agents, it ensures a purer taste, bringing out the natural flavors of each special ingredient.

Freshly Ground Black Pepper: essential in cooking as it releases aromatic oils and potent flavors elevating dishes with both warmth and complexity. Unlike pre-ground pepper, which may lose its potency over time, grinding peppercorns just before use ensures the fullest and most robust flavor profile. The act of grinding also allows for control over the coarseness, letting you tailor the pepper's texture to complement different dishes.

Nutritional Yeast: adds a nutty, cheesy flavor to food and can be used as a cheese substitute. Nutritional yeast is an unactivated version of the yeast used to make bread or beer. It has a savory or umami flavor, and may help lower cholesterol, boost your immune health, and more.

Egg Substitute

Flax-Based Egg Substitute: derived from ground flax seeds mixed with water, offer a nutritious and versatile alternative in plant based and baking recipes. The gel-like consistency of soaked flaxseeds mimics the binding properties of eggs, contributing a wholesome touch to dishes. Flax seeds are a nutritional powerhouse, packed with omega-3 fatty acids, fiber, and lignans, promoting heart health, digestive regularity, and overall well-being.

Grains

Arborio Rice: renowned for its plump and creamy texture, is a short-grain rice variety originating from Italy. With a high starch content, this rice is ideal for absorbing liquids, making it the star of classic Italian dishes like risotto. Its ability to release starch gradually during cooking results in a velvety consistency, creating a luxurious dining experience. Select a high quality, imported arborio rice to ensure a creamy, delicious outcome.

Farro: an ancient whole grain, boasts a nutty flavor and chewy texture that elevates both salads and grain bowls. Packed with fiber, protein, and essential nutrients like magnesium and B vitamins, farro not only supports digestion but also provides sustained energy. I love to swap out farro for white rice or pasta, it even makes a wonderfully robust and flavorful risotto.

Polenta: made from finely ground cornmeal, is not only a delicious comfort food but also a rich source of complex carbohydrates, fiber, and various essential nutrients, contributing to sustained energy and overall digestive health. Selecting the ideal cornmeal for your polenta is crucial for a mouthwatering outcome. Opt for a coarser grind if you crave a rustic texture, as it adds a delightful crunch to each bite. Conversely, a finer grind yields a smoother, creamier polenta, perfect for more refined palates.

Flower Chef's Hemp Seed Pasta: crafted with organic durum wheat semolina, organic hemp seed flour, and mineral water. This pasta delivers a perfect al dente texture, is packed with fiber and protein, and provides a balanced combination of omega-3 and omega-6 fatty acids. It adds a great texture and nuttiness, giving your dishes more body.

Plant-based Milks

Almond Milk: a versatile dairy alternative, lends a subtly nutty flavor and creamy texture to a myriad of recipes, from smoothies to baked goods. Its ability to seamlessly replace dairy makes it a go-to option for those with lactose intolerance or seeking a plant-based twist in their cooking. Rich in vitamins and minerals, almond milk offers a lower-calorie alternative with potential benefits for heart health and skin vitality.

Cashew Milk: pleases the palate with a subtle, nutty and creamy flavor, adding a touch of richness to your favorite recipes. Additionally, it stands out as a nutritious choice, offering a dairy-free alternative that is often fortified with vitamins D and B12, promoting bone health and energy metabolism.

Coconut Milk: when choosing coconut milk, opt for the full-fat, canned variety for a richer and more flavorful experience in cooking. Its velvety consistency and tropical undertones make it a delicious ingredient, adding depth to curries, desserts, and beverages with a distinctive coconut essence. Beyond its culinary appeal, coconut milk provides a dose of healthy fats, vitamins, and minerals, supporting everything from immune function to promoting skin health.

Hemp Milk: crafted from hulled hemp seeds and water, offers a plant-based alternative with a nutty flavor and creamy texture. This plant based milk is packed with omega-3 fatty acids, protein, and vitamins. I like to combine hemp milk with another plant based milk to balance out the grassy notes. It does add a nice clean green flavor that can help balance the sweetness of some nut milks or coconut milk.

Sweet

LorAnn Oils **Vanilla Bean Paste**: a fabulous alternative to vanilla extract. It packs full vanilla bean flavor, elevating any dessert with its elegance. When substituting vanilla bean paste for vanilla extract, use a 1 to 1 conversion.

LorAnn Oils **Orange Oil**: extracted from orange peels, is a concentrated burst of citrus flavor that immediately elevates culinary creations with its vibrant and zesty essence. Just a drop or two of orange oil adds a delightful pop, whether in dressings, baked goods, or savory dishes, infusing a refreshing and aromatic twist to dishes.

Flower Chef FOODS

FLOWER CHEF'S HEMP SEED PASTA

Crafted in Sicily with just three pure ingredients: organic durum wheat semolina, organic hemp seed flour and pristine water from the Nebrodi Mountain regions. This pasta delivers a perfect al dente texture, is packed with fiber and protein and provides a balanced combination of omega-3 and omega-6 fatty acids. Because of the Sicilian, low-temperature drying process, the gluten relaxes, making this pasta easier to digest than typical commercial alternatives. Additionally, it's made from hard ancient grains, resulting in a lower glycemic index compared to regular wheat pasta.

OLA GOURMET

Flower Chef Foods' line of gourmet hemp seed oil blends hemp seed oil with other oils making the miraculous hemp seed and its benefits more readily available in our diets. Each oil is meticulously crafted with purpose, featuring hand-selected ingredients sourced from local farms. There are currently four farm-to-bottle oils; OLIVE, TOAST, BRIGHT and SAVOR. Each flavor is created with intention and designed to add a flavorful drizzle and a healthy kiss to your culinary creations.

Scan to purchase and learn more about FlowerChefFoods.com

Also available on Amazon.

©Mehak Hussain

Ingredients

Premium Extra Virgin Olive Oil, Hemp Seed Oil

A true pantry staple, **OLIVE First Press OLA** combines premium extra virgin olive oil and hemp oil, creating a rich, robust flavor with notes of grassiness, pepper and a hint of fruitiness. Making it the perfect base for tasty vinaigrettes and nutritious dips. This versatile, timeless ingredient can also be drizzled over appetizers and main dishes as a finishing touch to liven up your cuisine.

Benefits

Extra virgin olive oil is rich in monounsaturated fat which lowers LDL (or "bad") cholesterol and total cholesterol; lowering the risk of heart disease and stroke. Observational studies have also shown that consuming higher amounts of olive oil can lower the risk of some cancers and even dementia. Extra virgin olive oil is not processed with high heat or chemicals and contains more of the natural vitamins and minerals that are found in olives, including vitamin E and vitamin K.

Ingredients

Walnut Oil, Hemp Seed Oil, Vanilla Bean

TOAST Vanilla Walnut OLA is an earthy toasted walnut oil blend with a touch of vanilla bean; adding a kiss of sweetness that reminds you of a warm cup of coffee. Toss with your favorite organic fruit, such as blackberries, as a welcome addition to desserts.

Benefits

Walnuts are particularly high in alpha-linolenic acid; a plant-based vegetarian source of the essential fatty acid omega-3. Among its numerous nutritional benefits, they also are a great source of fiber, potassium, magnesium and calcium. Walnuts have been linked to reduced risk of cardiovascular disease, help support weight loss and boost memory.

Vanilla beans are flavorful and nutritious. They are a good source of B vitamins and are a natural stress reliever and mood booster.

Ingredients

Almond Oil, Hemp Seed Oil, Orange Oil, Cardamom

Let **BRIGHT Orange Cardamom OLA** light up your meal as the flavors of citrus and cardamom spice magnificently play together to create a taste that is reminiscent of a beautiful summer day. Allow it to float on a yummy ginger-mint or lemon drop plum mocktail!

Benefits

Almonds are a highly nutritious nut that include vitamin E, fiber, calcium, magnesium and biotin. They offer many health benefits, including lowering LDL (or "bad") cholesterol levels and have been suggested to reduce the risk of heart disease.

Cardamom is an amazing ingredient that is used in both sweet and savory recipes. Studies have shown its antioxidant and diuretic properties could help lower blood pressure and it may help protect your liver.

Orange oil is made from the rind of an orange, which is extremely high in vitamin C and a great source of potassium and thiamin. Vitamin C supports a healthy immune system and improves the absorption of iron when consumed with plant-based foods rich in iron, such as leafy green vegetables.

Ingredients

Sesame Oil, Hemp Seed Oil, Mango Oil, Ginger Root

Bring life to your vegetarian cuisine with **SAVOR Sesame Ginger OLA**; a delightful combination of sesame and ginger that can be drizzled over plant-based appetizers such as carrot tater tots, or transformed into a delectable vinaigrette tossed with your favorite salad.

Benefits

Sesame oil is made from extracted sesame seeds, which are a small but mighty ingredient. These nutrient-dense seeds contain several vitamins that offer a wide variety of health benefits including iron, magnesium, vitamin B6, vitamin B12, vitamin K and folic acid. They also contain plant compounds that may lower cholesterol levels, and contain calcium and magnesium which are linked to improved blood pressure control.

Mango oil is derived from the mango fruit, which is rich in fiber, potassium and vitamins A and C. It can aid in digestion and may support eye health.

Ginger is a wonderful source of vitamin C, magnesium and potassium. It has been shown to provide pain relief, alleviate nausea and improve the regulation of blood sugar levels.

The Menu

MEDITERRANEAN BRUNCH

Mocktails
ROSEMARY GRAPEFRUIT MOCKTAIL
Florida grapefruit | green tea | ginger beer

BLOODY MARY MOCKTAIL
garden vegetable juice | horseradish | pickled vegetables

Amuse-Bouche
CITRUS BEET HUMMUS
blood orange | fresh thyme | cilantro oil

HOUSEMADE CROSTINI

First
CREAMY ASPARAGUS SOUP
roasted fennel | cashew cream | fresh chives

Second
KALE CAESAR SALAD
lacinato kale | shiitake mushroom bacon | focaccia crouton
pistachio butter Caesar dressing

Third
HEIRLOOM CARROT RISOTTO
toasted spices | roasted heirloom carrots | curried cashew cream

Sweet
CITRUS OLA OIL CAKE
Italian extra virgin olive oil | Meyer lemon curd

Make again? ♥

ROSEMARY GRAPEFRUIT MOCKTAIL

PREP 10 mins | SERVES 4

1 **grapefruit**, juiced

1 **grapefruit**, quartered

1 cup **green tea**

4 sprigs fresh **rosemary**

2 [12 oz] bottles **ginger beer**, chilled

Combine grapefruit juice, green tea and ice in a cocktail shaker.

Shake vigorously.

Strain into four ice-filled glasses and top with ginger beer.

Add a slice of grapefruit and a sprig of rosemary to each glass.

CHEF'S NOTES

This is a great base mocktail for anything citrus or mango. Try with lemonade for a jazzed-up Arnold Palmer. Muddle fresh mango in place of the grapefruit for an unexpected delightful drink!

Bloody Mary Mocktail Recipe >

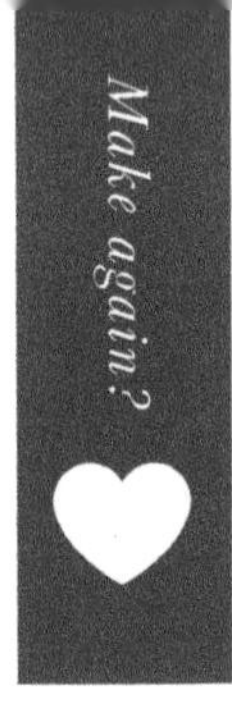

BLOODY MARY MOCKTAIL

PREP 10 mins | SERVES 4

3 oz **lemon juice**
2 tsp Worcestershire **sauce**
1 tbsp **horseradish sauce**
1 tsp **smoked paprika**
1 tbsp **celery salt**
freshly **ground black pepper**
2 tsp **Tabasco** *or* **Sriracha**
3 tbsp assorted **Pickled Vegetables**, *recipe page 23*
12 oz **garden vegetable juice**

GARNISH
4 stalks **celery**
4 **pickle spears**
1 **lime**, sliced into wedges
additional **pickled vegetables**

Also delicious with a splash of your favorite vodka!

In a small bowl, combine lemon juice, Worcestershire sauce, horseradish, celery salt, black pepper and Tabasco or Sriracha.

Toss combined liquids with assorted pickled vegetables.

Pour the tomato juice half way into four glasses filled with ice cubes.

Add the pickled vegetable mixture to each glass and stir vigorously to combine.

Top with remaining vegetable juice.

Garnish with the celery stalk, pickle spear and additional pickled vegetables.

Serve and enjoy!

CHEF'S NOTES

This mocktail is like a salad in a cup! Get creative with your salad mixture and toss in anything you like with the pickled vegetables. Favorites include: green beans, whole or crushed garlic cloves and green olives.

Anything goes in this recipe. Try pickling garlic cloves, roasted peppers or artichoke hearts to change things up.

PICKLED VEGETABLES

PREP 10 mins | SERVES 4

3 cups **assorted vegetables** [red onions, carrots, radishes, cucumbers, etc.], sliced thin

1 cup **filtered water**

½ cup **distilled white vinegar**

½ cup **apple cider vinegar**

3 tbsp **pure maple syrup** *or* **agave**

4 tsp **fine sea salt**

2 tsp **crushed red chili flakes**

Pack the vegetables into 1-pint mason jars or similar heat resistant containers.

In a small saucepan, combine the water, both vinegars, maple syrup, salt and crushed red chili flakes. Bring mixture to a simmer over medium-low heat, and carefully pour into the jars over the vegetables.

Use a spoon or spatula to press the vegetables down into the vinegar to release any air bubbles.

Let the pickled vegetables cool to room temperature for about 25 minutes before enjoying.

Cover and refrigerate leftover pickled vegetables to enjoy later.

CHEF'S NOTES

These are great to keep in the refrigerator to add to grain bowls, sandwiches, garden burgers and more.

These quick-pickled veggies are best when enjoyed within 3 days, but will keep for 1 to 2 weeks in the refrigerator.

Citrus Beet Hummus Recipe >

CITRUS BEET HUMMUS

PREP 15 mins | COOK 40 mins | MAKES 3 cups

2-3 small **red beets**

4 **garlic cloves**

2 sprigs **fresh thyme**

2 tbsp **olive oil**

kosher salt and **ground pepper** to taste

1 ½ cups cooked **chickpeas**, drained and rinsed

2 tbsp **tahini**

1 tbsp **fresh lemon juice**

2 tbsp **fresh orange juice**

2 tbsp **warm water**

1 tsp fresh picked **thyme**

1 tsp **cumin**

¼ cup **OLA Olive** *or* **extra virgin olive oil**

SERVE WITH

Herbed Crostini, *recipe page 29* and/or **fresh veggies**

Preheat oven to 400°F.

Place beets, garlic and sprigs of thyme together on a baking sheet lined with heavy duty aluminum foil. Salt and pepper liberally then drizzle with olive oil.

Place in oven and roast for 30 to 40 minutes or until the beets are fork-tender.

When beets have cooled, remove skins with a knife or use your hands and peel under running cool water.

Chop beets and place in a blender or food processor. Add the roasted garlic, chickpeas, tahini, lemon and orange juices. Add water and blend until smooth. Add cumin, thyme, salt and pepper. Mix ingredients to blend.

While blender or processor is blending, drizzle in olive oil and process until smooth and creamy.

To serve, drizzle with additional olive oil and fresh cilantro.

Serve with herbed crostini and fresh vegetables.

CHEF'S NOTES

This is one of my go to snacks! Not only is it absolutely delicious, but this recipe is high in: fiber, vitamin C, folate, vitamin B6 and magnesium.

A nice alternative to regular hummus or great served in a trio of dips alongside Whipped Lemon Hummus and Sun-Dried Tomato Caviar.

I love these with my Citrus Beet Hummus, recipe page 26.

HERBED CROSTINI

PREP 5 mins | COOK 10-12 mins | SERVES 6

1 **baguette**,
thinly sliced diagonally

½ cup **extra virgin olive oil**

flaky sea salt

cracked black pepper

2 tbsp **parsley**, finely chopped

2 tsp **rosemary**, **thyme**
or **oregano**, chopped

Preheat oven to 375°F.

Arrange the baguette slices in a single layer on a parchment lined baking sheet.

In a small bowl, combine olive oil, sea salt, black pepper, parsley and fresh herbs. Mix together thoroughly with a whisk or fork.

Liberally brush baguette slices with herbed oil.

Bake for 10 to 12 minutes or until golden and toasted.

Sprinkle with additional flaky sea salt and serve with desired toppings.

CHEF'S NOTES

These are great with crushed garlic and red chili flakes too!

Store in an airtight container at room temperature for up to two days.

Use OLA Toast or walnut oil, cinnamon and sugar for a sweeter version.

CREAMY ASPARAGUS SOUP

PREP 20 mins | COOK 1 hr | SERVES 6

3 tbsp **extra virgin olive oil**

1 large **onion**, finely chopped

kosher salt and **ground pepper** to taste

1 small bulb **fennel**, sliced thin

3 **garlic cloves**, finely chopped

1 **shallot**, finely chopped

1 tbsp picked **fresh thyme**

1 bunch local **asparagus**, chopped

2 qt **vegetable stock**

1 cup **Cashew Cream**, *recipe page 33*

2 cups **fresh baby spinach**

¼ cup **OLA Bright** *or* **favorite flavored oil**

Heat the oil in a large saucepan over medium heat. Add the onions, fennel, salt and pepper then cook for 5 minutes.

Add the asparagus, garlic, shallot, additional salt, pepper and red chili flakes. Sauté for about 15 minutes.

Add the fresh thyme and vegetable stock and simmer for 30 minutes.

Add the cashew cream and simmer for an additional 10 minutes.

Working in small batches, pour the soup into a blender and blend on high speed. Add the spinach to the last batch and continue blending until smooth. Pour the soup into a large sauce pan and stir to incorporate the spinach batch.

Ladle into small bowls and garnish with microgreens and additional cashew cream.

Drizzle with *OLA Bright* or your favorite flavored oil.

CHEF'S NOTES

For an elegant appetizer, serve this in shot glasses topped with long fresh chives and leek flowers.

Get creative, add dried dates or organic cane sugar and vanilla for a sweetened version.

CASHEW CREAM

PREP overnight *or* 1 hr soak | MAKES 1 cup

CASHEW CREAM BASE

1 cup **raw**, **unsalted cashews**

filtered water

⅛ tsp **kosher salt**

CURRY CASHEW CREAM

1 cup **raw**, **unsalted cashews**

filtered water

1 tbsp **curry**

1 tsp **lemon juice**, freshly squeezed

⅛ tsp **kosher salt**

CHEF'S NOTES

I love to have this on hand to add to soups, salads and dips. Add fresh garlic and plant-based Parmesan to make an incredible vegan Alfredo sauce for pasta!

SOAK THE CASHEWS

Place the cashews in a medium bowl.
Cover with filtered water.

Set aside uncovered at room temperature for 10 to 12 hours. Alternatively, cover cashews with boiling water and soak for 1 hour to speed up the process.

Drain the soaking water from the cashews and add them to blender.

Cover with fresh filtered water and salt.

If you're making Curry Cashew Cream, this is when you would add the curry and lemon juice.

Blend everything on high speed until completely smooth, about 3 minutes. Scrape down the sides of the blender with a rubber spatula and process again for 1 minute.

Use immediately or transfer to an airtight container and refrigerate for up to 1 week.

Add fresh chives, onion powder, fresh garlic and additional lemon juice for a yummy onion dip!

Kale Caesar Salad Recipe >

KALE CAESAR SALAD

PREP 20 mins | SERVES 6

4 cups **kale**, ribs removed, chopped

1 **red onion**, thinly sliced

1 cup shelled **pistachios**, roasted unsalted [¼ cup reserved for topping]

2 **garlic cloves**

2 tsp **lemon zest**

2 tbsp **lemon juice**, freshly squeezed

¾ cup **red wine vinegar**

1 cup **extra virgin olive oil**

kosher salt and coarsely **ground pepper**, to taste

1 tsp **crushed red chili flakes**

SERVE WITH

Shiitake Mushroom Bacon, *recipe page 39*

Homemade Sage Croutons, *recipe page 117*

Put chopped kale and thinly sliced red onion in a large bowl.

Put pistachios in a blender along with the garlic, lemon zest, lemon juice, red wine vinegar, crushed red chili flakes, salt and pepper. Blend on high speed until well mixed.

While blender is running, slowly drizzle in olive oil until dressing is thickened and emulsified.

Toss kale and onion with dressing until very well coated.

Add mushroom bacon and croutons. Toss again, reserving some of each for the top of the salad.

Serve salad on plates and top with extra pistachios, lemon zest, mushroom bacon and croutons.

CHEF'S NOTES

This is a great alternative to traditional Caesar salad. Try smearing dressing on a white plate and adding a small pile of salad next to it for an upscale, beautiful presentation.

Mushroom bacon is delicious in my Kale Caesar Salad, recipe on page 37.

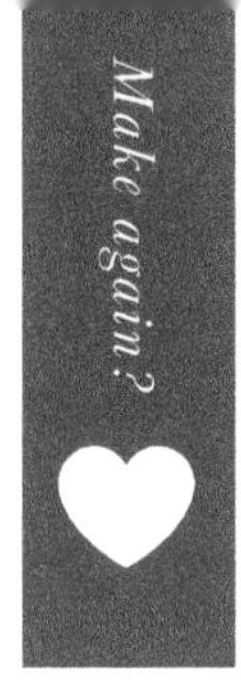

SHIITAKE MUSHROOM BACON

PREP 10 mins | COOK 30 mins | SERVES 6

8 oz **shiitake mushrooms**, stems removed

¼ cup **olive oil**

1 tsp **soy sauce** *or* **liquid aminos**

1 heaping tsp **fine sea salt**

¼ tsp **liquid smoke**

½ tsp **smoked paprika**

¼ tsp **cayenne**

CHEF'S NOTES

This recipe is also a fabulous addition to a plant-based Cobb salad with marinated chickpeas. I have a difficult time saving them for recipes, as I usually eat at least half of these beauties right out of the oven!

Mushroom bacon has the best texture the same day you cook it. However, you can store leftovers in an airtight container in the fridge for up to 5 days. I promise you, it won't last that long!

Preheat oven to 375°F and grease a large baking sheet with olive oil.

Slice the mushroom caps into ¼" thin slices.

Transfer the sliced mushrooms to a large bowl, toss them with the olive oil, soy sauce and seasonings. Use your hands to make sure they are coated evenly, massaging the liquid and seasonings into each piece.

Arrange coated mushrooms in a single layer on oiled baking sheet without overlapping any pieces.

Bake the mushrooms for 15 minutes. Use a fork to flip each slice over.

Return to the oven for 5 to 10 more minutes, until the mushroom bacon looks dark and golden. Be careful not to burn. The bacon will appear crispy on the edges, although the centers are still soft. They will crisp up even more as they cool.

Remove the mushroom bacon from oven and let cool on the sheet pan for about 15 minutes. Pat with a towel to remove any excess oil and serve.

Remember when slicing your mushrooms, thinner is better. This will ensure ultimate crispiness.

HEIRLOOM CARROT RISOTTO *with* CURRY CREAM

PREP 20 mins | COOK 30 mins | SERVES 8

4 cups **vegetable stock**

2 cups fresh **carrot juice**

2 tbsp **extra virgin olive oil**

1 large **yellow onion**, finely chopped

3 **garlic cloves**, chopped

1 tbsp **yellow curry**

1 tsp **ground cardamom**

½ tsp **crushed red chili flakes**

¼ tsp ground **anise**

1 ½ cups **arborio rice**

2 cups **dry white wine**

½ cup **nutritional yeast**

½ cup **Curry Cashew Cream**, *recipe on page 33*

kosher salt and **ground pepper** to taste

GARNISH

1 lb **heirloom carrots,** roasted

1 **lime**, sliced into wedges

¼ cup fresh **cilantro**, chopped

Drizzle **OLA Savor** *or* **toasted sesame oil**

Nutritional yeast is available in most grocery stores and makes an excellent substitute for cheese.

In a medium saucepan, bring the vegetable stock and carrot juice to a simmer. Set aside keeping warm.

In a large saucepan, heat olive oil. Add onion, garlic, curry, cardamom, chili flakes, anise and cook over medium-low heat. Stir continually, cooking until onions are softened and spices are toasted. Cook for approximately 5 minutes.

Add the arborio rice and sauté with the onion mixture for about two minutes, stirring frequently. Slowly pour in the wine, deglazing the pan. Season with salt and pepper and stir until all the wine is absorbed.

Stir in the warmed stock mixture, 1 cup at a time, stirring constantly and adding more stock once it has been absorbed. About 20 minutes total; the rice should be al dente and surrounded in a thick, creamy sauce.

Add the nutritional yeast and curried cashew cream. Season with salt and pepper and stir until creamy.

Garnish the risotto with roasted heirloom carrots, fresh lime and fresh cilantro. Delicious with a drizzle of *OLA Savor* or toasted sesame oil

CHEF'S NOTES

To add a bit of green, toss in fresh spinach or steamed fresh English peas.

Leftovers make unbelievable risotto cakes. Just add some flour and panko. Form into patties and sauté in olive oil. Serve with leftover cashew curry cream.

Play with the carrots in this risotto! Delicious with sliced roasted carrots stirred into the risotto. This is also a beautiful Spring side dish.

Citrus OLA Oil Cake Recipe >

Make again? ♥

The addition of orange oil sets this apart from traditional olive oil cake. A surprising kiss of orange will absolutely make a fan out of you!

CITRUS OLA OIL CAKE

PREP 30 mins	COOK 45 mins	SERVES 8-10

1 cup **good-quality extra virgin olive oil**, plus more for the pan

2 tsp *LorAnn Oils* **orange oil**

2 cups **all-purpose flour**, plus more for dusting the pan

1 tsp **kosher salt**

1 tsp **baking powder**

¼ tsp **baking soda**

1 ½ cups **granulated sugar**, *plus* 3 tbsp for sprinkling

4 **flax based eggs**

2 tbsp **lemon zest**, freshly grated

2 tsp **lemon juice**

2 tbsp **orange zest**, freshly grated

1 tbsp *LorAnn Oils* **vanilla bean paste**

1 ¼ cups **plant milk**, room temperature

¼ cup **icing sugar**

CHEF'S NOTES

This cake is absolutely incredible served with Plant-Based Meyer Lemon Curd, [*recipe page 47*] and whipped coconut cream.

One of my guilty pleasures is slicing this thin and toasting it for breakfast.

Preheat oven to 375°F. Grease a 9" round cake pan using extra virgin olive oil and line the bottom with parchment paper. Oil and flour the parchment lined cake pan, shaking out any excess flour.

In a large bowl, whisk together the flour, salt, baking powder and baking soda.

In the bowl of an electric mixer beat the sugar, flax based egg and both zests on high speed until fluffy and thick, about 5 minutes.

While the mixer is still running, slowly drizzle in the olive oil and orange oil. Beat until well incorporated for another 2 minutes.

Reduce speed to low and add plant milk and lemon juice.

Stir in flour mixture until just combined. Transfer the batter to the prepared pan. Smooth the top with a rubber spatula.

Sprinkle the top with remaining 3 tablespoons of sugar.

Bake the cake for approximately 40 to 45 minutes until a skewer inserted into the center comes out clean.

Transfer to a rack to cool for 20 minutes. Once the cake has cooled slightly, run a knife around the edge to release the sides of the cake from the pan.

Invert the cake onto a plate and then flip it back over onto the rack to cool completely.

Sprinkle with sifted icing sugar.

Store leftovers in an airtight container at room temperature for up to one week.

This recipe is an ode to OLA Bright which is made with a combination of almond oil, hemp seed oil and orange oil.

LORANN OILS
Orange
Oil

Make again?

PLANT-BASED MEYER LEMON CURD

PREP 5 mins	COOK 20 mins	MAKES 2 cups

1 [14-oz can] **coconut cream**

3 tbsp **Meyer lemon zest**

½ cup **Meyer lemon juice**

2 tbsp **arrowroot starch** *or* **cornstarch**

1-2 tbsp **pure maple syrup**, plus more to taste

CHEF'S NOTES

I love to serve this with Citrus OLA Oil cake, with fresh berry coulis and sweetened whipped cashew cream.

Place coconut cream and lemon zest in a small saucepan and whisk to combine.

Add lemon juice and arrowroot to a small mixing bowl and whisk to thoroughly dissolve. Add to the coconut cream mixture. Stir until combined.

Add maple syrup. Start with ½ tablespoon and increase to desired sweetness. Whisk again until well combined.

Place saucepan over medium heat, whisking often and bring to a simmer. Once mixture starts thickening, reduce heat to medium-low and continue cooking until a visible ribbon forms when scraping a spoon across the top. Curd should be thick and custard-like.

Let rest for 15 minutes, and whisk once more. Transfer to a glass bowl or jar. Cover with plastic wrap, making sure the plastic wrap touches the curd.

Refrigerate for at least 4 hours or overnight, until completely chilled and set.

This will keep in the refrigerator for 4-5 days.

The Menu

CHEF'S TABLE

Selection of Dips
CITRUS BEET HUMMUS *recipe page 26*
WHIPPED LEMON HUMMUS
SUN-DRIED TOMATO WALNUT CAVIAR

Tapas
CARDAMOM ROASTED CARROTS
onion marmalade | cardamom maple vinaigrette
toasted almonds | OLA Bright drizzle

STREET CORN
cilantro thyme brown butter | chipotle crema | fresh cilantro

TUSCAN PANZANELLA
shaved red onion | sweet yellow peppers | housemade croutons
OLA Olive infusion

HEMP SEED FLOUR PASTA
oven sweetened tomatoes | roasted garlic oil | crushed red chili flakes

Sweet
SUMMER PEACH CRISP
local peaches | maple almond spice | vanilla bean cashew ice cream

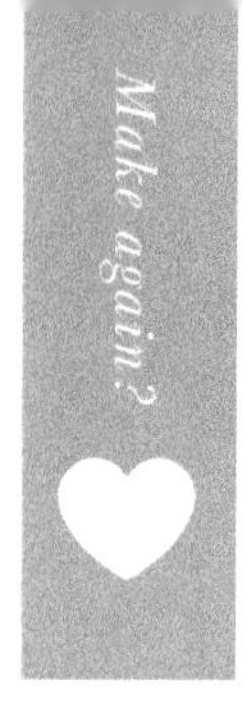

WHIPPED LEMON HUMMUS

PREP 10 mins | MAKES 3 cups

2 cans **chickpeas**, with liquid

5 **garlic cloves**, chopped

⅓ cup **lemon juice**, freshly squeezed [about 2-3 lemons]

⅓ cup **tahini**

2 tsp **cumin**

⅓ cup **OLA Olive**, *or* **extra virgin olive oil**

2 tbsp **filtered water**

kosher salt and **ground pepper** to taste

CHEF'S NOTES

I have this on hand all the time. Amazing smeared on a plate and used as a bed for cardamom roasted carrots. I snack on it during the day with fresh veggies and use it as a base for veggie sandwiches, garden burgers or falafel pitas.

Drain the chickpeas through a strainer into a bowl, reserving the liquid.

Add the chickpeas, ¼ cup of the chickpea liquid, garlic, lemon juice, tahini, cumin, salt and pepper to a food processor.

Whip on high speed, adding more liquid and scraping down the sides of the bowl for a total of 2 minutes. Add additional liquid until emulsified and smooth.

While the processor is running, drizzle in oil and slowly add water, a tablespoon at a time until the hummus is smooth and light in color. Season with salt and pepper. Taste and add more lemon juice or salt if needed.

You can serve the hummus when it is slightly warm or room temperature. Hummus can also be chilled for a firmer texture.

Whipping the hummus makes it light and airy but still velvety and rich. I like to form a well in the hummus and fill with additional oil and sprinkle it with smoked paprika and sea salt.

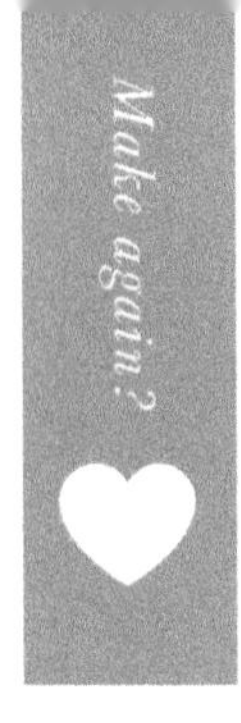

SUN-DRIED TOMATO WALNUT CAVIAR

PREP 15 mins | MAKES 2 cups

2 **roasted peppers**

⅓ cup **sun-dried tomatoes**, oil drained

½ cup **olive oil** *or* **oil from the sun-dried tomatoes**

2 **lemons**, juiced

3 **garlic cloves**, chopped

2 tsp **cumin**

1 tsp **smoked paprika**

1 ¼ cup **walnuts**, toasted and chopped

kosher salt and **ground pepper** to taste

GARNISH

Additional **olive oil**

2 tbsp fresh **cilantro**, chopped

In the bowl of a food processor, combine the roasted red peppers, sun-dried tomatoes, olive oil, lemon juice, garlic, cumin, paprika, half the walnuts and salt and pepper to taste.

Pulse until completely smooth and combined.

Stir in the remaining walnuts.

Spread the dip on a plate, drizzle with olive oil, and sprinkle with fresh chopped cilantro.

CHEF'S NOTES

To save time, purchase the roasted peppers at your local market.

Delicious served with toasted pita or flatbread. I love spreading this on a portobello mushroom burger or using it for a surprising twist on a roasted fennel tart.

CARDAMOM ROASTED CARROTS

PREP 15 mins | COOK 25 mins | SERVES 8

2 lbs **whole young carrots**, peeled, leaving some greens on top

¼ cup **olive oil**

1 tsp ground **cumin**

1 tbsp ground **cardamom**

1 tbsp **grated orange zest**

kosher salt and **ground pepper** to taste

GARNISH

1 cup **Maple Cardamom Vinaigrette**, *recipe page 59*

½ cup **Onion Marmalade**, *recipe page 57*

½ cup **cilantro**, chopped

1 cup slivered **almonds**, toasted

Position a rack in the center of the oven and preheat oven to 425°F.

Toss carrots in a bowl with olive oil, grated orange zest, cumin, cardamom, salt and pepper. Make sure carrots are evenly coated.

Spread evenly on a parchment lined, rimmed baking sheet. Transfer to the oven and roast. Turn carrots after 15 minutes and continue to bake until tender and golden-brown, about 25 minutes total. Carrots should still be firm but lightly caramelized.

While carrots are roasting, prepare onion marmalade and maple cardamom vinaigrette.

Remove the roasted carrots from the oven, toss with maple cardamom vinaigrette, onion marmalade and chopped cilantro. Taste and adjust seasoning with salt and pepper. Transfer to a large platter, top with toasted almonds and serve immediately.

CHEF'S NOTES

Oven roasting carrots intensifies their natural sweetness. Try swapping carrots for sugar in your savory recipes.

If you're feeling adventurous, try this:

Toast your own cardamom pods—the flavor is absolutely amazing! Place the cardamom pods into a medium skillet then place on the stove over medium heat. Stir frequently until lightly toasted, about 2 minutes. Transfer to a plate and allow to cool. Once cooled, transfer to a spice grinder and process into a fine powder, about 1 minute. For maximum freshness, use immediately!

Using red onions will produce a vibrant purple marmalade.

Make again?

ONION MARMALADE

PREP 10 mins	COOK 50 mins	SERVES 8

2 **onions**, thinly sliced
2 tbsp **extra virgin olive oil**
2 tbsp **apple cider vinegar**
1 tbsp **pure maple syrup**
1 tsp fresh **ginger**, grated
2 tsp **orange zest**
1 tbsp minced **thyme**
kosher salt to taste

Heat the skillet over low heat and add olive oil.

Add sliced onions and cook over a low heat, stirring frequently, until golden and caramelized for about 30 minutes.

Stir in apple cider vinegar, maple syrup, grated ginger, orange zest and fresh thyme. Cook until thick, about 20 more minutes.

Store this onion marmalade in a jar and use throughout the week.

CHEF'S NOTES

Delicious as a topping on a pizza or pasta. An absolute game changer in a vegan bowl. This can also be used as a filling for baked brie or as a compliment to an asparagus tart. Onion Marmalade immediately elevates any vegan charcuterie.

Make again?

MAPLE CARDAMOM VINAIGRETTE

PREP 5 mins | MAKES 1 cup

3 tbsp **pure maple syrup**

3 tbsp **sherry vinegar**

2 tsp **spicy Dijon mustard**

½ **orange**, juiced

2 tsp **ground cardamom**

½ tsp **ground anise**

¼ tsp **ground cumin**

¼ tsp **turmeric**

kosher salt and **ground pepper** to taste

½ cup **OLA Olive** *or* **extra virgin olive oil**

In a medium bowl, whisk together the maple syrup, vinegar, Dijon, orange juice, cardamom, anise, cumin, turmeric, salt and black pepper.

Slowly drizzle in the oil while whisking vigorously.

Keep this dressing tightly covered in the fridge to keep it fresh for up to 1 week.

CHEF'S NOTES

If you are unable to find sherry vinegar, apple cider vinegar can be used.

I like to keep a bottle handy for spinach salads, roasted squash or couscous salads.

STREET CORN *with* CILANTRO THYME BROWN BUTTER

PREP 15 mins | COOK 15 mins | SERVES 4-6

4 ears **corn**, shucked and halved

¼ cup **olive oil**

kosher salt and **ground pepper** to taste

2 tsp **ancho chili powder**, plus more for serving

3 medium **garlic cloves**, coarsely chopped

½ lb **plant-based butter**

1 cup **cilantro**, finely chopped divide into thirds

¼ cup fresh picked **thyme**

2 **limes**, cut into wedges

¾ cup **Chipotle Crema**, *recipe page 63*, divided

CHEF'S NOTES

When preparing for a party, I like to blanch the corn and prepare the crema the day before. Then, I heat the corn and toss with brown butter right before the event.

Preheat oven to 425°F. Blanch corn in salted boiling water until al dente, about 3 minutes.

Toss blanched corn in olive oil and season with garlic, ancho chili powder, salt and pepper. Bake for 5 minutes. Remove from the oven and transfer to a large bowl.

BROWNED BUTTER

In a small pot, simmer plant-based butter over low heat until browned, stirring occasionally to incorporate all of the brown bits. Once butter is browned and foam disappears, remove from heat.

Add ⅓ cup of the cilantro, thyme, salt and pepper. Mixture will bubble and foam and smell oh so delicious.

In a large bowl, toss corn with brown butter, ⅓ cup of the fresh cilantro and ½ of the chipotle crema.

Transfer to a platter and liberally drizzle with remaining chipotle crema along with remaining cilantro.

Serve with sliced limes on the side.

This recipe also makes an incredible corn salad if you take the corn off of the cobs. Toss with chopped red onion, arugula and black beans to have a wonderful meal.

*This corn is excellent grilled as well.
If doing so, blanch and grill cobs of corn
while whole and cut in half or thirds later.*

I love to keep this in my refrigerator.
Fabulous on sandwiches and wraps.
Game changer on avocado toast and tacos!

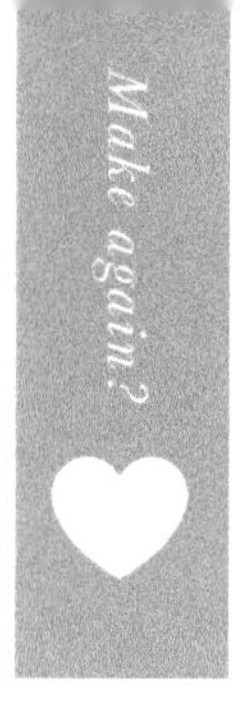

CHIPOTLE CREMA

PREP 10 mins | MAKES 1 ½ cups

½ cup **olive oil based mayonnaise**

¾ cup **tofu sour cream**

2 **chipotle peppers in adobo sauce**

½ **lime**, juiced

2 **garlic cloves**

2 tsp **cumin**

1 tsp **smoked paprika**

½ tsp **crushed red chili flakes**

kosher salt to taste

In a food processor, add the mayo, sour cream, chipotle peppers, lime juice, garlic, spices and a pinch of salt.

Process until the crema becomes smooth and creamy.

Add, salt, chili flakes and lime juice to taste.

Store it an airtight container and store it in the fridge for up to one week.

Thin slightly by emulsifying with olive oil, vinegar and water to make an unbelievable salad dressing for taco salad.

CHEF'S NOTES

Like all recipes, this crema's success hinges on achieving the ideal balance. If crema is too creamy, simply add more salt and lime juice or turn up the spice to fine-tune its flavor.

TUSCAN PANZANELLA

PREP 30 mins | COOK 15 mins | SERVES 8

2 ½ lbs **mixed ripe tomatoes**, cut into bite-size pieces

1 tbsp **kosher salt**, plus more for seasoning

1 **rustic sourdough baguette**, torn into 1 ½" cubes

12 tbsp **extra virgin olive oil**, divided

2 small **shallots**, minced [about 2 tbsp]

4 **garlic cloves**, finely chopped

2 tsp **Dijon mustard**

3 tbsp **white balsamic vinegar**

freshly ground **black pepper**, to taste

2 tsp **red chili flakes**

¼ cup **flat leaf parsley**, chopped

½ cup packed **basil** leaves, roughly chopped

CHEF'S NOTES

Use a hearty, open-structured bread, like ciabatta or sourdough.

Adjust oven rack to center position and preheat oven to 350°F.

Place chopped tomatoes in a colander set over a bowl and season with 2 teaspoons of kosher salt, toss to coat. Set aside at room temperature to drain, tossing occasionally. Let drain for a minimum of 15 minutes.

In a large bowl, toss bread cubes with 2 tablespoons of the olive oil. Transfer to a rimmed baking sheet. Bake for about 15 minutes until crisp and firm but not browned. Remove from the oven and let cool.

DRESSING

Remove colander with tomatoes from the bowl. Place the colander with tomatoes aside.

Using the juice from the tomatoes, add shallot, garlic, mustard and vinegar to the bowl. Whisking constantly, drizzle in remaining olive oil. Season dressing to taste with salt and pepper.

Combine toasted bread, tomatoes and dressing in a large bowl. Add basil leaves. Toss everything to coat and season with salt and pepper.

Let it rest for 20 to 30 minutes before serving and toss occasionally until the dressing is absorbed by the bread.

Be sure not to exceed 30 minutes before serving as panzanella will get soggy.

Hemp Pasta with Roasted Garlic Oil Recipe >

HEMP PASTA *with* ROASTED GARLIC OIL

PREP 10 mins | COOK 15 mins | SERVES 6

1 lb *Flower Chef's* **hemp seed pasta** *or* **protein packed penne pasta**

2 **garlic heads**, roasted and removed from skins

½ cup **extra virgin olive oil**

kosher salt and **ground pepper** to taste

1 tsp **crushed red pepper flakes**

¼ cup **flat-leaf parsley**, chopped

½ recipe **Oven Sweetened Tomatoes**, *recipe page 71*

CHEF'S NOTES

This pasta is wonderful served cold or at room temperature as well. To lighten it up for lunch, toss it with a cup of spinach dressed with olive oil and balsamic vinegar.

Feel free to add more olive oil at any point in this recipe.

Bring a large pot of cold water to a boil over high heat and salt generously. Add the pasta and cook. Stir occasionally until al dente, tender but not mushy, about 10 minutes.

In a small bowl, mash the roasted cloves of garlic with a fork until a paste forms. This can also be done in a food processor thinned out with 1 to 2 tablespoons worth of olive oil, for an even creamier texture.

While the pasta cooks, combine the roasted garlic paste, olive oil, salt, pepper and red pepper flakes in a large skillet and warm over low heat stirring occasionally, until the garlic emulsifies with the oil. About 5 minutes.

Reserve about a ¼ cup of the cooking water. Drain the pasta in a colander and add to the roasted garlic oil. Mix well.

Add the reserved water 1 tablespoon at a time, stirring continuously until a light sauce forms and the pasta is evenly coated. Add the parsley and oven sweetened tomatoes. Adjust seasoning, to taste.

Transfer to a large serving bowl or divide among 6 dishes. Top with additional parsley and olive oil.

These are incredible in pastas and on pizzas. Tomatoes immediately liven up any antipasto or veggie charcuterie board.

OVEN SWEETENED TOMATOES

PREP 15 mins | COOK 90 mins | SERVES 8

4 lbs **roma** *or* **heirloom tomatoes**, sliced in quarters lengthwise

2 tbsp **extra virgin olive oil**

1 tbsp **organic cane sugar**

2 tsp **kosher salt**

Preheat oven to 325°F.

Place sliced tomatoes in a large bowl and toss with olive oil, sugar and salt.

Place cut-side up on a parchment lined baking sheet.

Roast in oven until slightly dry but still juicy, approximately 60 to 90 minutes.

CHEF'S NOTES

Make these a day in advance and refrigerate. Bring to room temperature before serving.

Purée with equal parts of red wine vinegar and olive oil for a mouthwatering tomato vinaigrette!

Summer Peach Crisp Recipe >

SUMMER PEACH CRISP

PREP 20 mins | COOK 1 hr | SERVES 8

8 ripe **peaches**

1 tbsp **orange zest**

1 tbsp **lemon zest**

½ cup **pure maple syrup**

2 tsp **cinnamon**

1 tsp **ground nutmeg**

½ tsp **cloves**

2 tsp **vanilla extract**
or LorAnn Oils **vanilla bean paste**

1 tsp **almond extract**

TOPPING

1 ½ cups **flour**

1 cup **light brown sugar**, packed

½ tsp **kosher salt**

1 cup **organic oats**

½ lb cold **plant-based butter**, diced

CHEF'S NOTES

This is pretty much my most favorite breakfast in the world. So this is a must for your leftovers! Pop in a 400°F oven for 5 minutes for that fresh out of the oven taste.

Preheat oven to 350°F.

Butter a 9x14 by 2" deep rectangular baking dish.

Drop peaches into boiling water for one minute and remove with tongs. Peel peaches under cold, running water. Slice peeled peaches into wedges.

Combine the peaches with the zests, maple syrup, extracts and spices. Pour into a baking dish.

TOPPING

Combine flour, brown sugar, salt and oatmeal in a large bowl. Add cold butter and mix with pastry blender or fork until mixture is crumbly and the butter is pea sized. Scatter topping evenly over peaches.

Bake crisp for 45 minutes to 1 hour, until the top is brown and the juices are bubbly. Serve warm.

You can also make this recipe into individual ramekins and bake for 30 minutes. This makes a dinner party feel even more special.

Throughout the year, swap out the peaches for another fruit. This crisp topping is delicious on apples and berries as well.

The Menu

AUTUMN HARVEST SUPPER

Amuse Bouche
CREAMY PUMPKIN SOUP
star anise | cilantro | pomegranate

First
FORAGED MUSHROOM TART
fresh thyme | caramelized onions | crushed red chili flakes | spicy arugula

Second
SPINACH AND POACHED PEAR SALAD
red wine poached pears | spiced sugared pecans
pickled red onions | carrot cardamom vinaigrette

Third
STUFFED DELICATA SQUASH
spiced farro | dried cherries | slivered almonds
maple apple cider reduction | curry cashew cream

FLOWER CHEF'S SPECIAL DIPPING SAUCE
fresh baguette | fresh herbs | lemon | garlic chili oil

Sweet
CARAMEL APPLE UPSIDE DOWN CAKE
Washington apples | almond butter caramel | burnt sugar

I love to serve these in small tasting spoons as an amuse bouche. Just a couple elegant bites of this soup sets the palate for an array of Autumn flavors.

Creamy Pumpkin Soup Recipe >

Soup will definitely taste better the next day.
If you are entertaining guests, I highly recommend preparing a day ahead.

CREAMY PUMPKIN SOUP

PREP 30 mins | COOK 1 hr 30 mins | SERVES 8

¼ cup **olive oil**, divided

1 [4 lb] **sugar pie pumpkin**

2 fresh **leeks**, pale green and white parts only, chopped

4 medium **garlic cloves**, pressed

kosher salt and **ground pepper** to taste

2 tsp **curry powder**

1 tsp ground **cinnamon**

½ tsp ground **nutmeg**

½ tsp **crushed red chili flakes**

2 **star anise pods**

4 cups [32 oz] **vegetable broth**

½ cup fresh **apple cider**

1 cup **full fat coconut milk**

CHEF'S NOTES

To simplify this soup, substitute 3 cans of pumpkin purée [15 oz each] in place of the roasted pumpkin.

ROAST PUMPKIN

Preheat oven to 425°F and line a baking sheet with parchment paper.

Carefully cut the pumpkin in half and scoop out the seeds. Reserve the seeds to roast and use as garnish.

Slice each pumpkin half in half again to make quarters. Brush or rub 2 tablespoons of the olive oil over the flesh of the pumpkin and liberally season with salt and pepper. Place the quarters cut sides down, onto the baking sheet. Roast for 45 minutes or until the orange flesh is easily pierced with a fork. Set aside to cool.

SOUP

Heat the remaining olive oil in a large Dutch oven or heavy-bottomed pot over medium heat. Once the oil is shimmering, add leeks, garlic, salt, pepper and spices to the skillet. Stir to combine. Continue cooking, stirring occasionally for about 10 minutes.

While leeks and spices are cooking, peel the roasted pumpkin and discard the skin.

Add the pumpkin flesh, breaking it up with a wooden spoon. Season liberally with salt and pepper.

Make again? ♥

Pour in the vegetable broth and fresh apple cider. Bring the mixture to a boil. Reduce heat and simmer for about 15 minutes, allowing the flavors to come together and the soup to emulsify.

CURRIED PUMPKIN SEEDS

While the soup is cooking, pat the seeds dry. Toss with olive oil and kosher salt. Combine brown sugar and curry powder then toss with oiled pumpkin seeds. Roast for 15 minutes in a 400°F oven until lightly browned and fragrant.

Once the pumpkin mixture is done cooking, remove star anise and stir in the coconut milk. Remove the soup from the heat and let it cool slightly. Purée the soup with an immersion blender. If you prefer a creamier texture, a high speed blender working in batches will work best.

Taste the soup and add more seasonings as necessary.

Ladle the soup into individual bowls. Garnish with pomegranate seeds, curried pumpkin seeds and a dollop of plant-based sour cream. Also delightful with *OLA Bright* or a drizzle of extra virgin olive oil.

Let leftover soup cool completely before transferring it to a glass container and store in the fridge.

CURRIED PUMPKIN SEEDS

1 cup **pumpkin seeds**

2 tbsp **olive oil**

1 tbsp **brown sugar**

2 tsp **curry powder**

kosher salt

GARNISH

¼ cup **pomegranate seeds**

¼ cup **plant-based sour cream**

¼ cup **OLA Bright**
or **extra virgin olive oil**

curried pumpkin seeds

CHEF'S NOTES

This soup will keep in the fridge for up to 4 days or store in the freezer for up to 3 months.

Foraged Mushroom Tart Recipe >

FORAGED MUSHROOM TART

PREP 10 mins | COOK 30 mins | SERVES 8

1 sheet **prepared puffed pastry**

¼ cup **extra virgin olive oil**, divided

1 **sweet yellow onion**, sliced into ¼" half-moons

kosher salt and **ground pepper** to taste

16 oz [5 cups] **seasonal foraged mushrooms**, sliced [chanterelle, oyster, cultivated shiitake, or king trumpet]

4 **garlic cloves**, chopped fine

2 tbsp fresh **thyme**, chopped

½ tsp **crushed red chili flakes**

¾ cup chilled **Cashew Cream** *recipe page 33*

2 tbsp **flat-leaf parsley**, chopped

¼ cup **plant-based Parmesan**

GARNISH

2 cups fresh **arugula**

2 tbsp **extra virgin olive oil**

1 tbsp fresh **lemon juice**

kosher salt and **ground pepper** to taste

Preheat oven to 400°F.

Roll thawed puff pastry sheets to ¼" thickness. Score a frame into the dough leaving a one inch frame. Crimp edges with the tongs of a fork.

Brush the entire crust with 2 tablespoons of the olive oil and season with salt and pepper. Pierce the crust with a fork to create vents. This will prevent sogginess and help it stay crisp.

Set a wide skillet over medium-high heat and add remaining olive oil. When oil is wavy, add onions and season with salt and pepper. Continue stirring until onions soften and begin to brown, about 10 minutes. Remove onions and set aside.

Add the mushrooms, salt and pepper to the same pan and sauté over medium-high heat. Keep stirring, until softened and the mushrooms begin to brown slightly for about 5 minutes. Add garlic, thyme and red-pepper flakes, stir well and turn off heat.

Combine mushrooms and onions, set aside and cool to room temperature. Filling can be made several hours or 1 day in advance and stored in an airtight container in the fridge until ready to use.

Spread cashew cream over the pastry sheet, leaving the border exposed. Season with salt and pepper along with additional fresh thyme. Distribute onion-mushroom mixture evenly over the cashew cream. Dust with Parmesan and sprinkle with fresh parsley.

Make again? ♥

Bake until the pastry is crisp and golden. Be sure that the top of the mixture is lightly browned, about 25 minutes.

GARNISH

While tart bakes, toss arugula with olive oil, lemon juice, salt and pepper.

Slide baked tart onto a cutting board and pull away the parchment. Let it cool slightly before slicing into wedges. Top slices with dressed arugula and serve warm.

CHEF'S NOTES

For ease and convenience, I used frozen puff pastry for this recipe. There are so many delicious ones on the market and many of them are vegan! If you love your puffed pastry recipe go for it.

I'll often make two of these and put the second one in the freezer. So awesome and convenient to pop in the oven for last minute guests. Bake frozen tart for an additional 10 minutes.

Fresh pomegranate seeds also make this a beautiful addition to any holiday menu.

Make again? ♥

SPINACH *and* POACHED PEAR SALAD

PREP 10 mins | SERVES 6

¾ lb **baby spinach leaves**, rinsed and crisped

1 cup **Pickled Red Onions**, *recipe page 23*

3 **Red Wine Poached Pears**, sliced thin, *recipe page 88*

1 cup **Sweet and Spicy Pecans**, *recipe page 91*

1 tbsp **orange zest**

¼ cup **dried cranberries**

CARROT VINAIGRETTE

1 cup **extra virgin olive oil**

¾ cup **rice vinegar**

1 **orange**, juiced

1 **heirloom carrot**, peeled and cut into chunks

¼ **red onion**, peeled

¼ **yellow bell pepper**

1 tbsp **pure maple syrup**

3 tbsp fresh **thyme**

2 tsp ground **cardamom**

kosher salt and **ground pepper** to taste

In a large bowl, combine pears with spinach, pickled onions, pecans and orange zest. Season liberally with salt and pepper then toss to combine ingredients.

CARROT VINAIGRETTE

In the bowl of a high speed blender, combine the carrot, red onion, yellow bell pepper, maple syrup, ground cardamom, orange juice, rice vinegar, salt and pepper

Purée on high speed until well mixed.

With the blender on medium, slowly pour in the olive oil and blend until emulsified.

Pour over salad and gently mix to coat, adding additional salt and pepper to taste.

Garnish with extra pecans, dried cranberries and red wine poached pears.

For a holiday twist, substitute the orange juice in the vinaigrette, with a ¼ cup of reserved pear poaching liquid.

CHEF'S NOTES

I love to add avocado to this amazing salad.

Try adding plant-based ricotta and lemon zest for a twist.

RED WINE POACHED PEARS

PREP 5 mins	COOK 20 mins	SERVES 4 dessert / 8 salad

2 cups **dry red wine**
[such as cabernet or merlot]

3 tbsp **organic sugar**
or **pure maple syrup**

1 tbsp **orange zest**

4 firm, ripe **pears**

CHEF'S NOTES

If using pears for salad, reserve reduced poaching liquid for another use.

Poaching liquid can be reduced by half and used as a sauce for dessert.

These are so beautiful, sliced thin. Delicious in my spinach salad, recipe on page 87.

In a 4-qt saucepan, combine wine, sugar or maple syrup and orange zest. Bring to a boil, reduce heat and simmer for 5 minutes.

While liquid is simmering, peel pears, leaving the stem intact, being careful not to bruise the flesh of the pears. Slice half an inch off the bottom of the pears to create a flat surface.

Gently place pears in poaching liquid, cover and simmer for 20 minutes. Turn every 5 minutes to ensure even color until pears are cooked but still firm. Remove saucepan from heat, uncover and cool with pears upright in pan.

Once cool, cover and chill in the refrigerator for at least 3 hours or up to 24 hours, turning occasionally.

Gently remove pears from liquid and allow to come to room temperature before using.

This is amazing over plant-based vanilla ice cream.

SWEET AND SPICY PECANS

PREP 5 mins | COOK 15 mins | MAKES 5 cups

1 tbsp ground **cinnamon**

3 tbsp **light brown sugar**

1 tsp ground **cardamom**

½ tsp **cloves**

½ - 1 tsp **cayenne pepper**

kosher salt and **ground pepper** to taste

5 cups **pecan halves**

4 tbsp **plant-based butter**, melted *or* **OLA Toast** *or* **walnut oil**

CHEF'S NOTES

These are my ultimate go-to snacks. Keep on hand for oatmeal or granola, lunches, vegan charcuteries, as well as salads.

Preheat oven to 350°F.

Combine salt, pepper, cayenne, cinnamon and brown sugar in a small bowl.

Spread pecans on a large, rimmed baking sheet and toast for 10 minutes, until fragrant.

Transfer pecans to a large bowl and toss with melted butter or oil. Add spices and toss again to coat.

Return pecans to the baking sheet and toast until fragrant, for 3 to 4 minutes longer. Let cool.

Stored in an airtight container for a week or in the freezer for 3 months.

These amazing pecans are a fantastic addition to any special buffet. Bundled in a cellophane bag with a bow, they make a great hostess or holiday gift.

Stuffed Delicata Squash Recipe >

STUFFED DELICATA SQUASH

PREP 10 mins | COOK 30 mins | SERVES 8

4 large **delicata squash**

3 tbsp **apple cider vinegar**

¼ cup **olive oil**, divided

3 tbsp **pure maple syrup**

kosher salt and **ground pepper** to taste

1 small **onion**, chopped

1 cup **farro**

1 tbsp **mild curry powder**

2 tsp ground **cinnamon**

1 tsp ground **cardamom**

½ tsp **cayenne pepper**

3 cups **vegetable stock**

½ cup **dried cherries**

2 tbsp **orange zest**

1 cup loosely packed **flat leaf parsley**, chopped

½ cup **slivered almonds**, toasted

GARNISH

½ cup **Curry Cashew Cream**, *recipe page 33*

Preheat oven to 400°F. Cut each squash in half lengthwise. Scoop and discard the seeds. Arrange the halves on a sheet pan, flesh-side up.

Whisk together the vinegar, 2 tablespoons of the oil and the maple syrup in a cup. Brush the flesh side of the squash halves with the maple mixture and sprinkle with salt and pepper.

Place the squash flesh-side down in the baking dish and brush the skin side with maple mixture and sprinkle with additional salt and pepper. Place sheet on center rack and roast until the squash is fork-tender, about 20 minutes.

Remove from oven and poke the inside of the squash halves with a fork. Brush generously with more of the maple mixture.

Meanwhile, heat the remaining 2 tablespoons of olive oil in a medium saucepan over medium-high heat. Add the onions and cook, stirring occasionally, until soft and golden brown, about 6 minutes.

Add the farro, curry powder, cinnamon, cardamom, cayenne pepper and one teaspoon salt. Stir until the spices are toasted, about a minute.

Add the vegetable stock and bring to a simmer. Lower the heat, cover the pan, stirring occasionally, until the farro is tender and most of the liquid is absorbed, about 10 minutes. Remove from the heat and let it sit, covered, for 5 minutes.

Make again?

Uncover and stir in the dried cherries, orange zest, remaining maple mixture, half of the parsley and half of the almonds.

Stuff the squash halves with the farro. Cover with foil and heat for 10 minutes (20 to 30 minutes if chilled).

Laddle warmed curry cashew cream over squash and garnish with additional parsley and almonds.

Serve warm or at room temperature.

CHEF'S NOTES

The squash may be baked and stuffed the day before and refrigerated. To reheat, cover the baking dish loosely with foil and reheat in a 350°F oven for about 20 minutes.

For a delicious twist, switch out the almonds for pistachios.

This is a showcase for your oil of choice, so be sure to choose the highest quality.

Make again?

FLOWER CHEF'S HERBED DIPPING SAUCE

PREP 5 mins | MAKES 1 ¼ cup

1 cup **extra virgin olive oil** *or* **OLA Olive**

kosher salt and **ground pepper** to taste

1 tbsp **lemon juice**, freshly squeezed

1 tbsp fresh **parsley**, finely chopped

1 tbsp fresh **rosemary**, finely chopped

2 **garlic cloves**, crushed

1 tbsp **lemon zest**

1 tsp **crushed red chili flakes**

Dry herbs can be used and garlic omitted for an oil that can be stored for up to a month, refrigerated. A great holiday gift!

Pour oil into a shallow bowl. Season with salt and pepper.

Top with parsley, rosemary, lemon juice, garlic, lemon zest and crushed red chili flakes.

Leave the herbs on top, to swirl into each bite with a bit of oil. This will give maximum flavor per bite.

Serve with your favorite crusty breads!

Store leftovers in a tightly covered jar in the fridge for up to one week.

CHEF'S NOTES

Use this oil as a palette to create your own masterpiece! I love to switch it up and add different oils, vinegars or spicy mustard along with a dash of sriracha or horseradish. Change the feel of the dip based on your cuisine of choice.

CARAMEL APPLE UPSIDE DOWN CAKE *with* BURNT SUGAR

PREP 15 mins | COOK 1 hr | SERVES 8-10

APPLES

1 tbsp **brown sugar**

1 tsp ground **cinnamon**

2 large or 3 small **apples**, peeled, cored and sliced ½" thick

CAKE

Cooking spray

2 cups **organic all-purpose flour**

1 tsp **baking powder**

1 tbsp ground **cinnamon**

1 tsp **nutmeg**

½ tsp **cloves**

1 tsp **kosher salt**

½ cup [1 stick] **plant-based butter**, softened

1 cup **organic sugar**

½ cup **brown sugar**, lightly packed

4 **flax based eggs**

1 tbsp *LorAnn Oils* **vanilla bean paste**

¾ cup **plant milk**

GARNISH

Almond Butter Caramel, *recipe page 101*

Preheat oven to 350°F and grease an 8" round cake pan with cooking spray.

Toss apples with cinnamon and brown sugar. Layer in a circle on the bottom of the prepared cake pan.

In a large bowl, whisk together flour, baking powder, cinnamon, nutmeg, cloves and salt. Set aside.

In the large bowl of a stand mixer, beat together butter and sugar until softened. Add flax based eggs one at a time, stir to combine. Stir in vanilla bean paste.

Add half the dry ingredients to wet ingredients, beating until just combined.

Pour in plant milk and mix until fully incorporated. Add remaining dry ingredients and stir until just combined.

Pour batter over apples and bake until a toothpick inserted into the middle comes out clean, about 1 hour.

Remove from oven. Let cool in pan for 15 minutes. Invert the cake by gently flipping it onto a cooling rack and remove the pan. Let cool completely.

Before slicing, sprinkle one tablespoon of sugar onto the cooled cake. Burn sugar with a kitchen torch and serve immediately with almond butter caramel.

CHEF'S NOTES

If only serving a few people, you can sprinkle a small amount of sugar on each slice and torch individually.

I love to make a pool of caramel sauce in the center of a dessert plate and serve the cake on top with a scoop of vanilla bean cashew ice cream. Yum!

This is the most amazing vegan caramel and it comes together in about 5 minutes! Store in an airtight glass jar for a week. This makes a wonderful gift.

ALMOND BUTTER CARAMEL

PREP 5 mins | COOK 5 mins | MAKES 1 ¼ cups

½ cup **coconut oil**

½ cup **pure maple syrup**

¼ cup **almond butter**

1 tsp *LorAnn Oils*
vanilla bean paste

sea salt

Melt the coconut oil and maple syrup together over low heat in a small saucepan, stirring occasionally.

Whisk in the almond butter for about 2 minutes until fully incorporated and very smooth.

CHEF'S NOTES

This caramel will separate a bit when stored. Reheat for 1 minute in the microwave, stir well and the sauce will come together again.

Love to pool this on dessert plates and top with apple upside down cake or dark chocolate cupcakes.

The Menu

A CELEBRATION OF WINTER

Amuse Bouche

ROSEMARY CASHEWS
fresh rosemary | sea salt | cracked pepper

First

EGGPLANT CAPONATA
crushed tomatoes | yellow bell peppers | capers

HERBED POLENTA
fresh rosemary | extra virgin olive oil

Second

TOMATO CREAM SOUP
roasted garlic | shredded carrots | fresh basil

Third

PUMPKIN CAESAR SALAD
grilled baby romaine | brown butter sage croutons | toasted pepitas
pumpkin caesar dressing

Fourth

FRENCH MEATLESS PIE
foraged mushrooms | yukon gold potatoes | fresh herbs

FRESH GREEN BEAN CASSEROLE
crispy onions | mushroom cream

Sweet

DARK CHOCOLATE CUPCAKES
cocoa | vanilla bean | fig fudge frosting

HOMEMADE IRISH CREAM
whiskey | espresso | dark chocolate syrup

ROSEMARY BROWN BUTTER CASHEWS

PREP 5 mins	COOK 10 mins	MAKES 2 cups

1 lb **roasted unsalted cashews**

3 tbsp **plant-based butter**

3 tbsp fresh **rosemary**, chopped

1 tsp **cayenne pepper**

1 tsp **light brown sugar**

sea salt and **ground pepper** to taste

CHEF'S NOTES

Brown butter is amazing. The recipe can be doubled, and half can be stored in the fridge or freezer for later use.

Great on squash risotto or a seasonal tart.

Store in a covered glass container in the fridge for up to one week.

Preheat oven to 350°F.

BROWN BUTTER

Add plant-based butter to a thick-bottomed skillet over medium heat. Slicing the butter in equal pieces will allow it to melt more evenly. Whisk frequently.

Once melted, the butter will foam up a bit, then subside. Lower the heat and watch closely, as lightly browned specks begin to form at the bottom of the pan. The butter should have an amazing nutty aroma. Careful not to overcook!

Remove butter from heat, let cool.

CASHEWS

Spread the cashews on a rimmed sheet pan and place in the oven until warm, about 5 minutes.

Add the rosemary, cayenne, sugar and salt to the browned butter.

Add the warm cashews to the butter mixture and simmer over low heat for one minute, tossing in the frying pan to combine. Serve while still warm.

These cashews are unbelievable and despite the quick preparation, will be the hit of your holiday party!

Caponata is a traditional Sicilian dish. I love it served as an appetizer on crostini toast, flatbread or small bites of polenta.

ITALIAN EGGPLANT CAPONATA

PREP 30 mins | COOK 25 mins | SERVES 8

1 large **eggplant**, diced into ½″ cubes

kosher salt

2 tbsp **extra virgin olive oil**

1 **yellow onion**, chopped

1 **red bell pepper**, cored and diced

2 small **celery stalks**, thinly sliced

3 **garlic cloves**, chopped

black pepper

1 cup **crushed tomatoes**

¼ cup **capers**

1 tbsp **organic sugar** *or* **agave**

1 tsp **crushed red pepper flakes**

¾ cup **red wine vinegar**

¼ cup **flat leaf parsley**, chopped

¼ cup fresh **oregano**, chopped

2 tbsp fresh **basil**, cut into ribbons

Season the eggplant cubes with salt and set aside in a colander for 30 minutes. This will prevent eggplant from tasting too bitter. Pat dry with a paper towel.

Heat half the olive oil in a large sauté pan over high heat until it begins to smoke slightly. Add eggplant and quickly sauté for 1 to 2 minutes until browned but still firm. Remove from the pan.

Add remaining olive oil to the skillet and add the onions, bell pepper and celery. Season with kosher salt and black pepper. Cook for 5 minutes, tossing frequently until softened. Add the garlic and sauté for an additional minute, stirring to incorporate.

Add the tomatoes, capers, sugar or agave and crushed pepper flakes. Pour in red wine vinegar and stir to combine. Simmer over medium-low heat for 10 minutes.

Stir in the cooked eggplant and simmer for an additional 5 minutes, until the caponata comes together.

Finish with fresh parsley, basil ribbons and additional olive oil.

CHEF'S NOTES

If preferred, eggplant can be roasted in an oven at 400°F for 20 minutes.

Also delicious as a main course served with lots of crusty bread and Caesar salad.

This is definitely a comfort food meal. Delicious topped with foraged mushrooms or oven sweetened tomatoes and caramelized onions found in this book.

Herbed Polenta Recipe >

HERBED POLENTA

PREP 15 mins | COOK 35 mins | SERVES 8

8 cups **water**

1 tsp **fine salt**

2 cups **polenta**

4 tbsp **extra virgin olive oil**, divided

½ cup **assorted fresh herbs**, chopped [parsley, thyme, oregano, rosemary, sage]

¼ cup **nutritional yeast**

CHEF'S NOTES

Switch up the herbs and get creative!

Plant-based butter can be used in place of the olive oil. This will produce a creamier, richer finished product.

Bring water and salt to a boil in a large saucepan; pour polenta slowly into boiling water, whisking constantly until there are no lumps.

Reduce heat to low and simmer, whisking often until polenta starts to thicken, for about 5 minutes. Polenta mixture should still be slightly loose.

Cover and cook for 30 minutes, stirring frequently. When the polenta is too thick to whisk, stir with a wooden spoon. Polenta is done when the texture is creamy and the individual grains are tender.

Turn off heat and gently stir 2 tablespoons of the olive oil into polenta until incorporated. Add nutritional yeast and chopped herbs, reserving 2 teaspoons for garnish. Stir to combine. Cover and let stand for 5 minutes to thicken.

Stir polenta and transfer to a serving bowl.

Top polenta with remaining 2 tablespoons olive oil and additional herbs of your choice.

If making into cakes, spread cooled polenta onto a well oiled, parchment lined sheet pan. Wrap tightly and store in the fridge overnight. Using a pastry cutter or a sharp knife, cut into desired shape.

Serve chilled, sautéed in olive oil or oiled, seasoned and roasted in a 400°F oven for 15 minutes.

Makes a great appetizer when cut into cakes and topped with Italian Eggplant Caponata, recipe page 107.

TOMATO CREAM SOUP

PREP 5 mins | COOK 1 hr | SERVES 8

¼ cup **extra virgin olive oil** *or* **OLA Olive**

1 **yellow onion**, diced

4-5 **garlic cloves**, chopped fine

¼ cup **tomato paste**

2 [28 oz] cans **whole tomatoes**

1 large **carrot**, grated

2 tsp **crushed red chili flakes**

3 tbsp fresh **oregano**, chopped

2-3 sprigs fresh **basil**, left whole

6 cups **vegetable stock**

½ cup **Cashew Cream**, *recipe page 33*

kosher salt and **ground pepper** to taste

GARNISH

¼ cup fresh **basil**, sliced in ribbons

additional **extra virgin olive oil** *or* **OLA Olive**

Heat olive oil in a large, non-reactive sauce pan. Add onion and garlic. Cook until the onion is completely soft and translucent, about 10 minutes.

Increase heat to medium-high; add tomato paste. Continue cooking, stirring often, until paste has begun to caramelize, about 5 minutes.

Add the tomatoes and their juices to the pot, breaking them up with your fingers or a wooden spoon. Add shredded carrot, chili flakes, oregano, basil and vegetable stock to the pot. Increase heat to high, then bring to a simmer. Season liberally with salt and pepper. Reduce heat to medium. Simmer until flavors come together and soup has reduced by half, about 45 minutes.

Remove soup from heat and discard basil sprigs. Using an immersion blender, purée the soup. Stir in cashew cream. Simmer the soup until flavors meld, around 10 to 15 minutes longer. Season to taste with additional salt, pepper and herbs. Add more cashew cream, if desired.

Serve with a drizzle of *OLA Olive* or extra virgin olive oil, fresh basil ribbons, salt and pepper.

CHEF'S NOTES

This soup is so fabulous with plant-based grilled cheese in the winter.

Dress it up: serve with homemade sage croutons topped with melted plant-based Parmesan.

Pumpkin Caesar Salad Recipe >

Grilling the romaine adds an unexpected savory twist to this salad. Serve while slightly warm to bring all the flavors together.

PUMPKIN CAESAR SALAD *with* SAGE CROUTONS

PREP 5 mins | COOK 20 mins | SERVES 8

SAGE CROUTONS

6 slices **grainy sourdough bread** *or* **crusty French bread**, torn into 1″ pieces

3 tbsp **extra virgin olive oil**

4 tbsp fresh **sage**, chopped

kosher salt and **ground pepper** to taste

DRESSING

½ cup **pumpkin purée**

¼ cup **extra virgin olive oil** *or* **OLA Bright**

¼ cup fresh **lemon juice**

1 tbsp **Worcestershire sauce**

kosher salt and coarsely **ground pepper**, to taste

1 head **romaine lettuce**

1 tbsp **olive oil**

kosher salt and **ground pepper** to taste

GARNISH

½ cup **pepitas**

sage croutons

CROUTONS

Preheat oven to 400°F.

On a large-rimmed baking sheet, toss all crouton ingredients until evenly coated. Bake for 5 minutes, then toss and bake for 8 minutes longer, until light brown and crispy. Set aside.

DRESSING

In a small bowl, mix all dressing ingredients. Set aside.

SALAD

Brush full romaine lettuce with 1 tablespoon of olive oil and season with salt and pepper.

Grill romaine over medium high heat turning every 2 minutes. Grill for a total of 6 minutes then remove from heat and allow to cool.

If tossing salad, combine romaine, croutons, pepitas and dressing in a large bowl. Toss to coat and serve immediately.

If enjoying with a knife and fork, mound whole romaine leaves on a plate, drizzle with dressing and top with croutons and pepitas.

CHEF'S NOTES

The pumpkin dressing is also amazing in a plant-based Cobb salad or in a grain bowl with fresh spinach, brown rice and grilled tofu.

French Meatless Pie Recipe >

When I was growing up, my family had French Meat Pie every Christmas Eve. The original recipe came from my grandmother. I've now added a reimagined version as a tradition to our own family Christmas Eve meal.

FRENCH MEATLESS PIE

PREP 35 mins | COOK 1 hr | SERVES 8

6 oz **meatless ground beef***

1 **onion**, finely chopped

1 ½ lbs **assorted foraged mushrooms**, sliced [chanterelle, oyster, cultivated shiitake, porcini, king trumpet]

3 **garlic cloves**, chopped

1 tbsp **Worcestershire sauce**

2 tsp **steak seasoning**

2 large **potatoes**, cooked and mashed

kosher salt and **ground pepper** to taste

2 tbsp **flat leaf parsley**, finely chopped

1 tbsp fresh **thyme**, finely chopped

2 tsp fresh **sage**, finely chopped

1 **double crust pie crust**

1 tbsp **plant milk**

CHEF'S NOTES

*Alternative to meatless beef option; use additional mushrooms like portobello.

Traditionally this dish is served with ketchup. I love to top it with chipotle crema and truffled ketchup. This is also delicious with a bit of my fig jam or Italian eggplant caponata.

Preheat oven to 450°F.

Combine meatless ground beef and chopped onion in a large, preheated and oiled frying pan. Over medium heat, brown the mixture for about 5 minutes, stirring frequently.

Add the mushrooms along with garlic. Stir to combine and sauté for an additional 6 minutes or until mixture is cooked through.

Add Worcestershire, steak seasoning, breadcrumbs, fresh herbs, salt and pepper. Mix well to combine.

Stir mashed potatoes into meatless mushroom mixture. Make sure they are well incorporated. Season with additional salt and pepper.

On a lightly floured surface, use a rolling pin to roll each crust into an 11" circle.

Line a glass pie dish with one crust and fill with prepared filling, making a large mound in the center. Cover with the remaining pastry, fluting the edge and cutting several vents on top.

Brush the top crust with plant milk to help brown.

Bake for 60 minutes or until heated through. If crust starts to darken too much, cover edges with foil tents.

For an elegant holiday party, this recipe can be divided into 6 large ramekins for a more formal feel.

This is a plant-based take on a childhood favorite.

GREEN BEAN CASSEROLE

PREP 10 mins	COOK 25 mins	SERVES 8

1 ½ lb fresh **green beans**, trimmed and halved

2 tbsp **olive oil**

1 **yellow onion**, diced

1 lb **mushrooms**, sliced

3 **garlic cloves**, minced

3 tbsp organic **all-purpose flour**

2 tsp fresh **thyme**

¾ cup **vegetable broth**

1 ¼ cup **plant milk**

1 tsp **onion powder**

½ tsp **crushed red chili flakes**

kosher salt and **ground pepper** to taste

2 cups **fried onions**, divided

CHEF'S NOTES

For a quick easy hack: use 4 cups of prepared plant-based mushroom soup in place of the flour, vegetable broth, plant milk and mushrooms. Add the onions and seasonings to the soup before combining all ingredients together.

Preheat oven to 400°F.

Bring a large pot of salted water to a boil. Blanch green beans for about 4 minutes or until bright green and slightly tender. Drain and rinse well with cold water.

Heat 2 tablespoons of olive oil in a large, oven safe skillet over medium heat. Add onion and mushrooms. Sauté for 5 minutes. Keep stirring frequently until onions are translucent and mushrooms start to brown. Add the garlic and sauté for an additional 2 minutes, stirring often.

Sprinkle the flour over the onion mixture, stirring to evenly incorporate. Let brown for a couple of minutes. Add in the fresh thyme and continue stirring throughout the process.

Slowly add broth, whisking into the roux until smooth. Add plant milk and continue to whisk. Add onion powder, chili flakes, salt and pepper. Bring sauce to a simmer then allow it to thicken, about 5 minutes. Adjust the seasoning with salt and pepper.

Stir in green beans and ½ cup crispy onions until evenly coated in sauce. Top the casserole with remaining onions and bake for 15 minutes or until sauce is bubbling and onions have browned.

Remove from the oven, allow to cool for about 10 minutes before serving.

Make again?

DARK CHOCOLATE CUPCAKES *with* FIG FUDGE FROSTING

PREP 15 mins | COOK 40 mins | SERVES 12

2 cups **organic flour**

2 cups **organic sugar**

¾ cup **dark cocoa powder**

2 tsp **baking soda**

1 tsp **baking powder**

1 tsp **kosher salt**

2 **flax based eggs**

1 cup **strong coffee**, cooled

1 cup **plant milk** *combined with*
1 tbsp **apple cider vinegar**

½ cup **plant-based vanilla yogurt**

2 tsp *LorAnn Oils* **vanilla bean paste**

FROSTING

Fig Fudge Frosting, *recipe page 126*

Preheat oven to 350°F.

Line, spray or grease and flour a regular sized cupcake pan. Set aside.

In a large bowl, combine the dry ingredients; flour, sugar, dark cocoa powder, baking soda, baking powder and salt. Mix well.

Add wet ingredients; flax based eggs, strong coffee, plant milk with apple cider vinegar, plant-based vanilla yogurt and vanilla bean paste to the dry ingredients. Whisk to combine.

Pour into prepared muffin pan.

Bake for 35 to 40 minutes or until an inserted toothpick comes out clean.

Frost with homemade fig fudge frosting.

CHEF'S NOTES

This recipe makes the best cupcakes in the world! Be sure to use a dark roast coffee, brewed strong. The coffee will intensify the chocolate notes and bring depth and roundness to the flavors.

FIG FUDGE FROSTING

PREP 10 mins | FROSTS 1 cake / 12 cupcakes

1 ½ cups [3 sticks] **plant-based butter**, chilled

1 cup **Fig Jam**, *recipe page 129*

2 tsp *LorAnn Oils* **vanilla bean paste**

4 cups **powdered sugar**, divided

½ cup **dark cocoa powder**

2 tbsp **plant milk**, divided

In the bowl of a stand mixer, combine half the powdered sugar, plant-based butter and 1 tablespoon of plant milk. Mix on medium speed until ingredients come together.

Add the rest of the sugar, the cocoa powder and whip on high for 4 minutes until a thick buttercream forms (stopping a couple of times to scrape down the sides of the bowl with rubber spatula). Stir in remaining plant milk.

Add the vanilla bean paste and fig jam. Mix on medium speed for another minute, making sure all ingredients are completely incorporated.

Make sure plant-based butter is chilled when making this recipe. The frosting will have a better texture and will emulsify more effectively.

CHEF'S NOTES

Adding the powdered sugar in phases helps the frosting to be more manageable.

It is very important to whip the ingredients for at least the recommended time so that enough air is worked into the buttercream. This will give the frosting the best texture possible!

This jam is delicious on a savory tart or spread on flatbread or sandwiches.

FIG JAM

PREP 5 mins	COOK 40 mins	MAKES 1 ½ cups

1 lb fresh **figs**

½ cup **organic sugar**
or **pure maple syrup**

¼ cup **water**

½ **orange**, juiced

2 tsp *LorAnn Oils*
vanilla bean paste

CHEF'S NOTES

Careful not to burn yourself, this jam is very hot and can splatter a bit.

This is a quick jam and not meant to be stored at room temperature. It will keep in the fridge for ten days or frozen for three months.

This recipe is the mouthwatering secret ingredient in my Fig Fudge Frosting! *Recipe page 126*

Pull the stems off the figs and chop into quarters.

Purée the figs in a food processor until mostly smooth. Leave a few chunks remaining to give texture to the jam.

Transfer the fig paste to a medium-sized heavy-bottomed (but not cast iron) pot. Stir in the sugar, water and orange juice. Bring to a boil over medium-high heat then, reduce heat to medium.

Boil, stirring constantly, until the texture becomes jam-like. Mixture will be shiny and will fall off the spoon in bigger clumps or sheets, as opposed to small drips.

Remove from the heat and stir in vanilla bean paste.

Carefully transfer the jam to a clean jar. Let it cool completely, uncovered (about an hour or so), before sealing with the lid and transferring to the fridge.

Several years ago I developed this plant-based version and found I liked it more—it tends to be a bit lighter.

HOMEMADE IRISH CREAM

PREP 15 mins | MAKES 24 oz

1 cup **plant-based creamer**

1 can [14 oz] **plant-based sweetened condensed milk***

1 ½ cups **good quality Irish whiskey**

1 tbsp **instant espresso powder**

¼ cup **dark chocolate syrup**

1 tbsp *LorAnn Oils* **vanilla bean paste**

In a high speed blender, combine plant-based creamer, plant-based sweetened condensed milk, Irish whiskey, instant espresso, dark chocolate syrup and vanilla bean paste.

Blend on high for 30 seconds.

Store in a tightly sealed container in the refrigerator.

Shake well before serving.

CHEF'S NOTES

*If you can't find plant-based sweetened condensed milk, you can make your own by combining 1 can of full-fat coconut milk and ⅓ cup granulated sugar. Simmer over medium-low heat for 45 minutes or until liquid is reduced by half.

I have been making this for holiday gifts for the past several years. People look forward to receiving it and return their glass bottles every year in hopes of receiving a full bottle the next holiday season. This has become a wonderful Houser Family Tradition.

Flower CHEF

ACKNOWLEDGEMENTS

In the lush garden of gratitude, I find myself surrounded by the vibrant blooms of support and collaboration. Writing this plant-based cookbook has been a journey filled with love, flavor and the incredible warmth of shared passion. It takes a community to create something this special. I am eternally grateful to the amazing people who have transformed this project into a reality.

To My Beloved Family: Your unwavering encouragement and endless love have been the soil in which my culinary dreams take root. Special thanks to my husband Jim and our two sons who cheer me on every day. Thank you for being the roots that anchor me and the sunshine that brightens my every endeavor. To my mom, who always follows the recipe, thank you for following these and for sharing your seasoned perspective.

Creative Director Extraordinaire: To our visionary creative director, Krista Murphy, who sprinkled a touch of magic on every page. Your artistic flair and keen eye for detail have turned these recipes into visual feasts. Your beautiful brain has the ability to transform what lives in my mind into the pages of a book. Thank you for making the book as visually delightful as the dishes within.

The Photographic Maestro: Capturing the essence of each dish in a single frame is an art. Sarah Hays, our photographer, has mastered this art. Your lens has brought out the beauty in every leaf, every grain and every vibrant hue of the plant-based palette. The visuals speak volumes, and it's all thanks to your incredible skill.

Wordsmith Editor: A big shout out to the wordsmith behind the scenes, Mehak Hussain, our editor. Your meticulous editing has polished this cookbook into a literary gem. Your steadfast commitment to holding this project together has been grounding for all of us. You have been the glue. Thank you for ensuring that every word and flavor is perfectly balanced.

The Dedicated Team: A heartfelt appreciation to the amazing team at Flower Chef Foods. Mike Hayes, Scott Berman and KC Thompson; your support supercharges me everyday. Your confidence in me and belief in my craft fuels my enthusiasm. I am blessed to have a team of such dear friends. Each one of you has added a unique spice to this culinary adventure.

Culinary Collaborators: To the fellow culinary enthusiasts who contributed their expertise and innovative ingredients—thank you for adding an extra layer of flavor to this collection. We extend our sincere gratitude to *LorAnn Global* for including their US-produced products in our diverse array of ingredients. This cookbook is a tapestry woven with the threads of our combined passion for plant-based goodness.

The Beauty Team: A special thanks goes out to the incredibly talented hair and makeup team who added a touch of glamor to this culinary adventure from behind the scenes. To Rachel Katherine Gilbert, Donna Rae and Victoria Windsor. Your exceptional skills not only elevated my appearance but also filled each moment with radiant beauty, making this journey truly extraordinary. Your contributions are truly appreciated.

Readers and Future Plant-Based Enthusiasts: Last but certainly not least, to you—the ones who will embark on this gastronomic adventure. May these plant-based recipes bring joy to your tables and inspire your inner artist, creating special communal moments for the people you love to feed. These are the moments to savor in life.

In the garden of gratitude, each one of you is a unique and irreplaceable bloom. Thank you for making this cookbook a celebration of flavors, love and shared experiences.

With love and gratitude,

Jules

The Flower Chef

INDEX

Printed in the USA
CPSIA information can be obtained
at www.ICGtesting.com
LVHW071915080224
771348LV00011B/174